First DIRECTIONS

BASIC READING SKILLS

John Cooper

Oliver & Boyd

Contents

Oliver & Boyd
Longman House
Burnt Mill
Harlow
Essex CM20 2JE

A Division of Longman Group Ltd

© Oliver & Boyd 1989

First published 1989

ISBN 0 05 004465 6

Set in Linotron Helvetica Medium 14 on 20 pt
Produced by Longman Group (F.E.) Ltd
Printed in Hong Kong

Acknowledgements
Illustrations by Tim Archbold, Janet Blakely,
Michael Charlton, Robert Geary, Dermot Power,
Joanna Williams

1. The Alphabet

First letters

The alphabet is a set of 26 letters:

abcdefghijklmnopqrstuvwxyz

I. Look at the pictures.
   Say what they show.

d

c

2. Look at the letter below each picture.
   Write the two letters in the order you find them in
   the alphabet.
3. Write the whole word for each picture.

   c _ _   d _ _

There is a letter beside each picture.

c

b

In your own book do the following.

I. (a) Write the letters in alphabetical order: b _

(b) Write the whole word for each picture: car _ _ _

(c) Write the words in alphabetical order: bus _ _ _

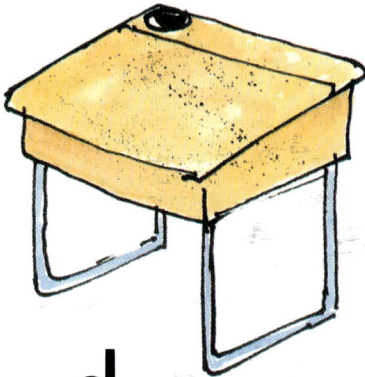

d

c

2. (a) Write the letters in alphabetical order: c _

(b) Write the whole word for each picture: desk _ _ _ _

(c) Write the words in alphabetical order: c _ _ _ _ _ _ _ _

3. Write the words in alphabetical order. (Look at the first letters.)

s

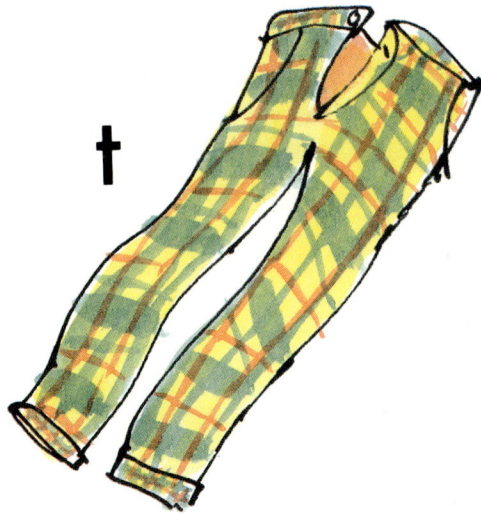

t

s _ _ _   t _ _ _ _ _ _ _

4. Write the words in alphabetical order.

o

b

l

o _ _ _ _ _   b _ _ _ _ _   l _ _ _ _

abcdefghijklmnopqrstuvwxyz

1. Write the whole words in alphabetical order: h _ _ _ _   c _ _

2. Write the whole words in alphabetical order: s _ _ _   f _ _ _

3. Write the words in alphabetical order: s _ _ _ _   f _ _   b _ _

What's next?

abcdefghijklmnopqrstuvwxyz

We must remember the order of letters. If you look in your dictionary you will see that the words are written in alphabetical order.

Below are eight sections. In each section there are three lines and in each line a letter is missing.

Write the answers in your own book. Write the missing letter only. The first one in each section is done for you.

1. d ?
   Answer: e
   h ?
   k ?

2. p ?
   Answer: q
   t ?
   v ?

3. k ?
   Answer: l
   n ?
   r ?

4. m n o ?
   Answer: p
   b c d ?
   w x y ?

5. d e f ?
   Answer: g
   k l m ?
   p q r ?

6. f g h i ?
   Answer: j
   c d e f ?
   r s t u ?

Vowels

abcdefghijklmnopqrstuvwxyz

There is a letter beside each picture below – u a o e i.
These letters are called **vowels**.

umbrella

apple

orange

egg

ice-cream

The letters are not in the order you find them in the alphabet.

l. Write them in the order in which they come in the alphabet:

    a _ _ _ _   That is what we call their alphabetical order.

2. Write the whole word for each picture:

    umbrella a _ _ _ _   o _ _ _ _ _   e _ _ i _ _ _ _ _ _ _ _

3. To put the words into alphabetical order we must put their
   first letters into alphabetical order. Write the words in alphabetical
   order:

    apple e _ _ i _ _ _ _ _ _ _ _   o _ _ _ _ _   u _ _ _ _ _ _ _

Codes

Damian has written in a secret code. He used numbers for the vowels. (Every word has at least one vowel.)

1bcd2fgh3jklmn4pqrst5vwxyz

This is what Damian wrote:

> 3 w2nt t4 sk3 3n th2 1lps l1st y21r

Look at the code. 1 stands for **a**.

Write out the whole message, beginning I w _ _ _ _ _ _ _ _

Lesley has written in a different code. She has used a number for every letter.

a	b	c	d	e	f	g	h	i	j	k	l	m
1	2	3	4	5	6	7	8	9	10	11	12	13

n	o	p	q	r	s	t	u	v	w	x	y	z
14	15	16	17	18	19	20	21	22	23	24	25	26

This is what Mary wrote:

> 13 25   2 9 18 20 8 4 1 25   9 19   15 14   13 15 14 4 1 25

Look at the code.   13 stands for **m**
                     25 stands for **y**
                     2 stands for **b**

Write out the whole message, beginning: My b _ _ _ _ _ _ _ _ _

9

2. Skim and Scan

Index

Below is an index. It is in alphabetical order. We often find an index at the end of a book. It tells us the page to look up. For instance, bear is on page l7.

bear   page l7

giraffe   page 9

camel   page l3

hippopotamus   page l5

elephant   page 4

kangaroo   page 20

lion   page 12

tiger   page 22

monkey   page 1

zebra   page 5

Answer the questions below. The first one is done for you.

On which page can you read about:

1. giraffe?   *Answer:* page 9
2. monkey?
3. hippopotamus?
4. zebra?
5. elephant?

Meg's Week on the Farm

On which page could you read about:

1. ponies?   *Answer:* 34

2. wheat?

3. cows?

4. milk?

5. tractor?

6. butter?

7. the farmer?

They Went to Explore

Look at the index. On which page could you read about:

1. Columbus? *Answer:* l7
2. USA?
3. Magellan?
4. India?
5. Pacific?
6. Livingstone?

Contents

How can you tell what is in the box?
A contents list will show you.

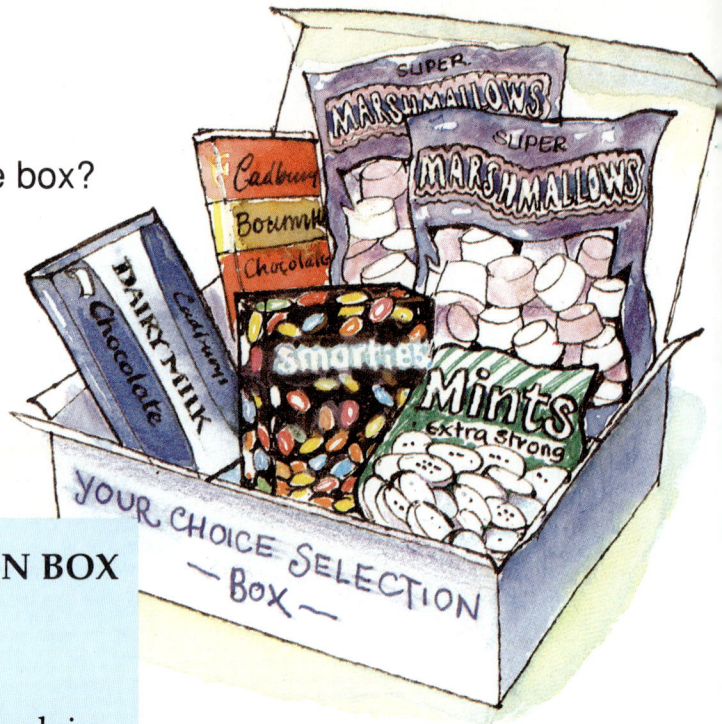

YOUR CHOICE SELECTION BOX

Contents

Chocolate: 1 bar milk, 1 bar plain
Smarties: 1 box of 60
Mints: 1 packet
Marshmallows: 2 packets

The contents list tells you what is in the selection box.

Answer YES or NO for the questions below. (The first one is done for you.) Look at the contents list each time.
Does the selection box contain:

1. toffee?   *Answer:* No
2. mints?
3. fruit gums?
4. milk chocolate?
5. marshmallows?
6 Twix?
7. Smarties?

A book may have a contents list at the beginning. It tells you what is in the book and the page where you will find it.

BOOK OF STORIES

Contents

Look at the contents list above and answer these questions.
(The first one is done for you.)

1. How many stories are there in the **BOOK OF STORIES**?
   Answer: 4

2. Does the book have the story **Tiny Terror**?

3. Does it have the story **Sinbad the Sailor**?

4. On which page would you find **Monster Monday**?

5. Use the contents list at the front of this book (page 2) and answer these questions:
   (a) On which page will you find **Main Ideas**?
   (b) On which page will you find **Information**?
   (c) On which page will you find **Clues**?

3. Main Ideas

Labels and Headings

Labels
Write in your own book what the pictures show.

Begin like this: Children are _____.

Children in the _____.

1. Write one word to tell
   what you see in the picture.

2. Write one word to tell
   what you see in the picture.

3. Write one word to tell what you see in the picture.

4. Write one word to tell
   what you see in the picture.

Headings

Sometimes a heading tells us the main idea in what we are reading.

Here are four lines of pictures.

1.

Write a heading for each line, like this: 1. Pumps

2.

3.

4.

I.

green medium red
small large blue

In your book write these words
under two headings like this:

sizes	colours
medium	green

2.

shoes slippers cap
helmet hat
socks boots bonnet

In your book write these words
under two headings like this:

footwear	headgear
shoes	cap

3.

bread rolls chops bacon
newspapers envelopes cake
sausages comics

Write these words under
headings like this:

butcher	baker	stationer
chops	bread	newspapers

Titles

Titles are put in to help us to find what we want to read about.

Below we see the title **Rescued by Helicopter**. If we are interested we may read on. If not, we may decide to read something else.

Rescued by Helicopter

An injured climber was lifted to safety yesterday. Alice Ennals had hurt her leg in a fall when climbing

Below are three titles and the beginnings of three stories. Copy down the first title, **Speed Record on Roller Skates**.

Choose the beginning of the story which matches and write it underneath the title. Do the same for each of the others.

Titles

Speed Record on Roller Skates

School Pet Show

More Caravan Holidays in the Highlands

Beginnings of Stories

Evan Davies yesterday won first prize in a roller skating race. He also received an extra prize for finishing the race faster than anyone else had ever done.

More and more children are taking up roller skating because ...

Pupils are to bring their pets to school on Friday afternoon. This will be their first-ever pet show.

Some are worried about too many pets being together in the playground at the same time. They fear that...

There are to be more sites for caravans in the west Highlands.

Many people like caravan holidays because ...

Perhaps your teacher will allow you to finish each story.

Sentences

Sometimes a sentence tells us one main thing which is more important than the rest.

Read each sentence and then write the answer to the question underneath. The first one is done for you.

1. Jane learned wind-surfing when she was on holiday.

 What is the main thing that sentence 1 tells us?
 Is it: (a) that Jane learned wind-surfing?
 or   (b) that Jane was on holiday?
 Answer: Jane learned wind-surfing.

2. She became very good at keeping her balance, although she sometimes fell.

 What is the main thing that sentence 2 tells us?
 Is it: (a) that she sometimes fell?
 or   (b) that she became very good at keeping her balance?

What is the most important idea in each sentence? Is it (a)
or (b)? The first one is done for you.

1. (a) Snow began to fall at midnight   (b) when no-one expected it.

   Answer: (a) Snow began to fall at midnight.

Do the following in the same way:

2. (a) The children all enjoyed   (b) although it was
         playing in the snow   very cold.

3. (a) They built a snowman   (b) which was one metre high.

4. (a) When the rains came   (b) the snow was all washed away.

Read each sentence and then write the answer to the question underneath. The first one is done for you.

Cars

1. Although some people go past your school on bicycles, most people pass in cars of different colours and different makes.

   What is the main thing sentence 1 tells us?
   Is it that   (a) a few people cycle past?
   or   (b) most pass in cars?
   Answer: most pass in cars.

2. The Mini is a cheap car to run because it does not use much petrol, but it has little room for luggage.

   What is the main thing sentence 2 tells us?
   Is it that (a) the Mini is cheap to run?
   or   (b) there is little room for luggage?

3. An estate car, which is a different shape, is much bigger and has much more room for people and for luggage.

   What is the main thing sentence 3 tells us?
   Is it that   (a) the estate car has a different shape?
   or   (b) the estate car has more room?

Paragraphs

Guy Fawkes Night

Read paragraphs (a), (b), (c) and (d) below and then answer the questions.

Number 1 is done for you.

(a) A few men planned to kill King James I. They were going to blow up the Houses of Parliament on 5 November when he was there.

(b) One of these men was Guy Fawkes. He stored barrels of gunpowder ready in a cellar underneath.

(c) On 4 November a search was made. Guy Fawkes was arrested beside the gunpowder and later put to death.

(d) Ever since that time bonfires have been lit on Guy Fawkes Night. Stuffed figures called guys are burned on the fires.

Which paragraph is about:
1. bonfires on Guy Fawkes Night? *Answer:* (d)
2. the plan to kill King James I?
3. the arrest of Guy Fawkes?
4. Guy Fawkes storing the gunpowder?

Helicopters

Below are four paragraphs about helicopters.

You will see that each paragraph starts a new line. Read the four paragraphs.

A. A helicopter has rotor blades. These blades can make the helicopter go up, down or forward.

B. Helicopters can fly fast or very slowly. They can also stay still in the same position.

C. Rescues are often carried out by helicopters. They are useful in land rescues, as in mountains, or at sea.

D. Police often use helicopters when they are making searches. They also use them to watch crowds and to help to control traffic.

All the paragraphs tell us about helicopters.

Each paragraph is telling us something different about helicopters.
Read them again and see if you can spot what is the main
idea in each paragraph.
Number 1 is done for you.

1.   Do the sentences in paragraph A tell us about:

    (a) what the rotor blades can do?

    or

    (b) the speed of helicopters?

    Answer: (a) what the rotor blades can do.

2.   Do the sentences in paragraph B tell us about:

    (a) how helicopters can fly?

    or

    (b) the size of helicopters?

3.   Do the sentences in paragraph C tell us about:
    (a) the cost of helicopters?

    or

    (b) rescues by helicopter?

4.   Do the sentences in paragraph D tell us about?

    (a) people going on holiday by helicopters?

    (b) how helicopters land?

    or

    (c) how police use helicopters?

4. Information

Pictures

We often read to find things out.

We also find things out by looking at pictures.

Below you see pictures of a camp site in March, May, July and December.

Look at the pictures carefully and answer the questions below.

March

May

July

December

1. In which month did no campers come? Can you think why?

2. In which month did most campers come? Can you think why?

3. Did more campers come in March than in May?

Graphs

We can find things out by looking at graphs.
Look at the pictures below and then answer the questions underneath.

In our class

spent their summer holidays at home

spent their summer holidays away from home

1. How many pupils are there in the class?
2. How many spent their holidays at home?
3. How many spent their holidays away from home?

We could also give the information on page 29 like this:

Holidays at home

Holidays away from home

Number of pupils

1. How many pupils are there in the class?
2. How many spent their holidays at home?
3. How many spent their holidays away from home?

Some children in the class take part in sports.
Some swim, some ski, some skate and some run.
The graph below tells you all you need to know so that you can
answer the questions.

Sports We Take Part In

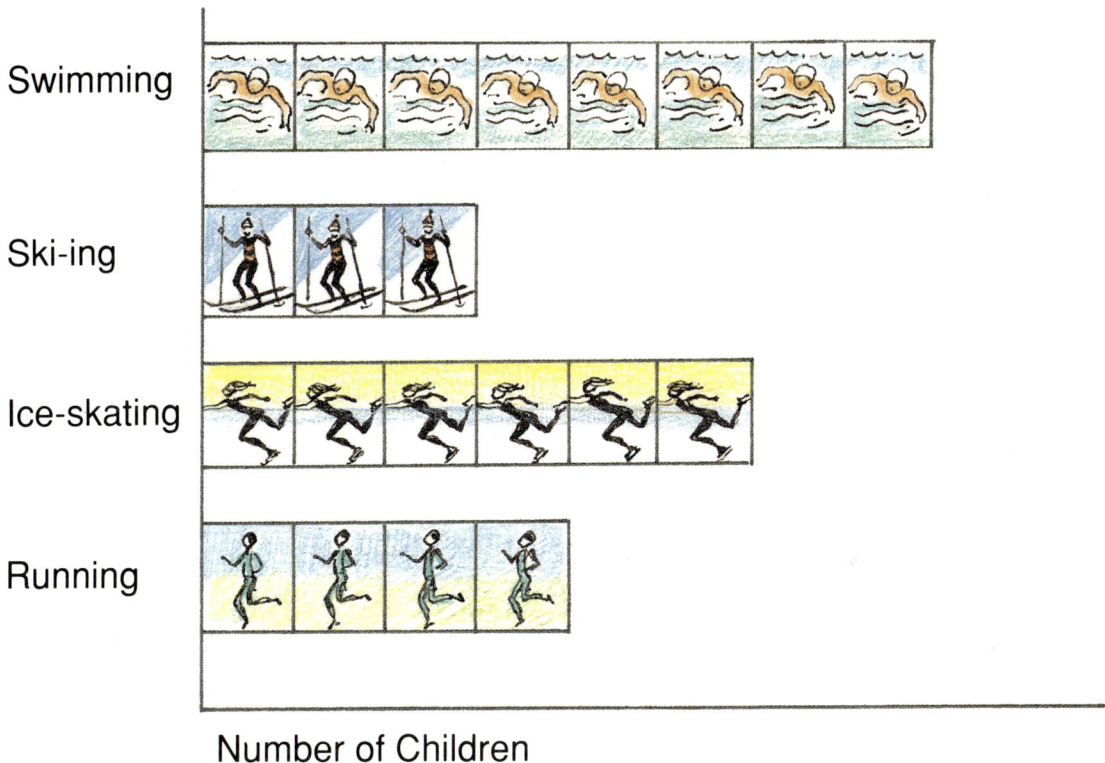

Number of Children

1. Which is the most popular sport?
2. Which is the least popular sport?
3. How many take part in running?
4. How many children altogether take part in these four sports?
5. If there are 25 pupils in the class, how many do not take
   part in any of these four sports?

Below there is a graph. It tells us the kinds of ice-cream children in the class like best.
Look at it carefully and then answer the questions below.

The Ice-Cream We Like Best

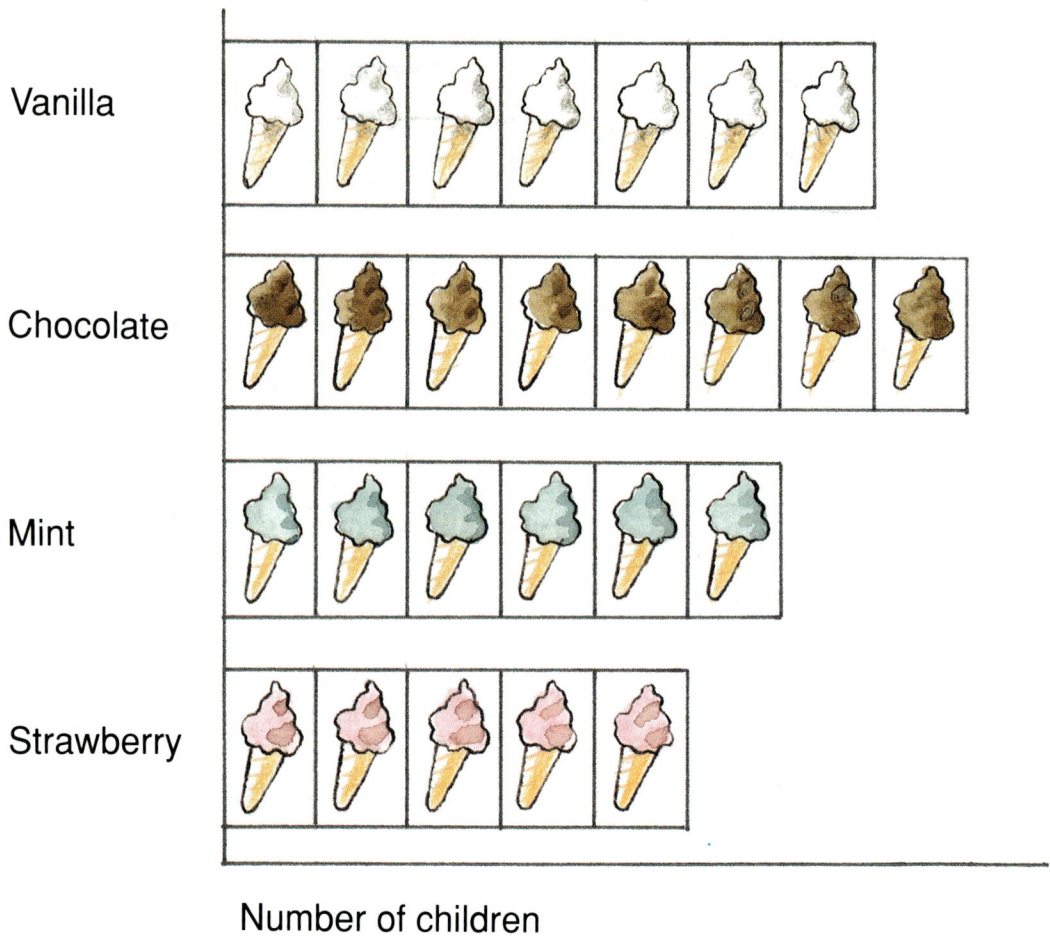

Number of children

1. Which is the favourite ice-cream?
2. Which is the least popular ice-cream?
3. How many pupils like mint ice-cream?
4. More like chocolate ice-cream than strawberry ice-cream. How many more?

Road Signs

Some signs give us orders.

For example, this sign means no cyclists allowed.

Mr Gray wished to park his car in the centre of Donmuir.
Study the signs and try to work out the answers to the
questions.
Number 1 is done for you.

1. Why did he not park at A?
   Answer: There is a **no waiting** sign.
2. Why did he turn left at B?
3. Why did he slow down at C?
4. Why did he park at D?

33

Some signs are there to warn us.

Mrs Layton was driving to the airport to meet some friends. She saw warning signs which made her drive very carefully in some places.

There were signs warning her of: low flying aircraft,
cattle crossing,
road works,
children crossing,
falling rocks.

Look carefully at each sign and then answer the questions.

1. Why did she drive carefully at A?

   Answer: She saw a road works sign.

2. Why did she drive carefully at B?

3. Why did she drive carefully at C?

4. Why did she drive carefully at D?

5. Why did she drive carefully at E?

35

Street Plan

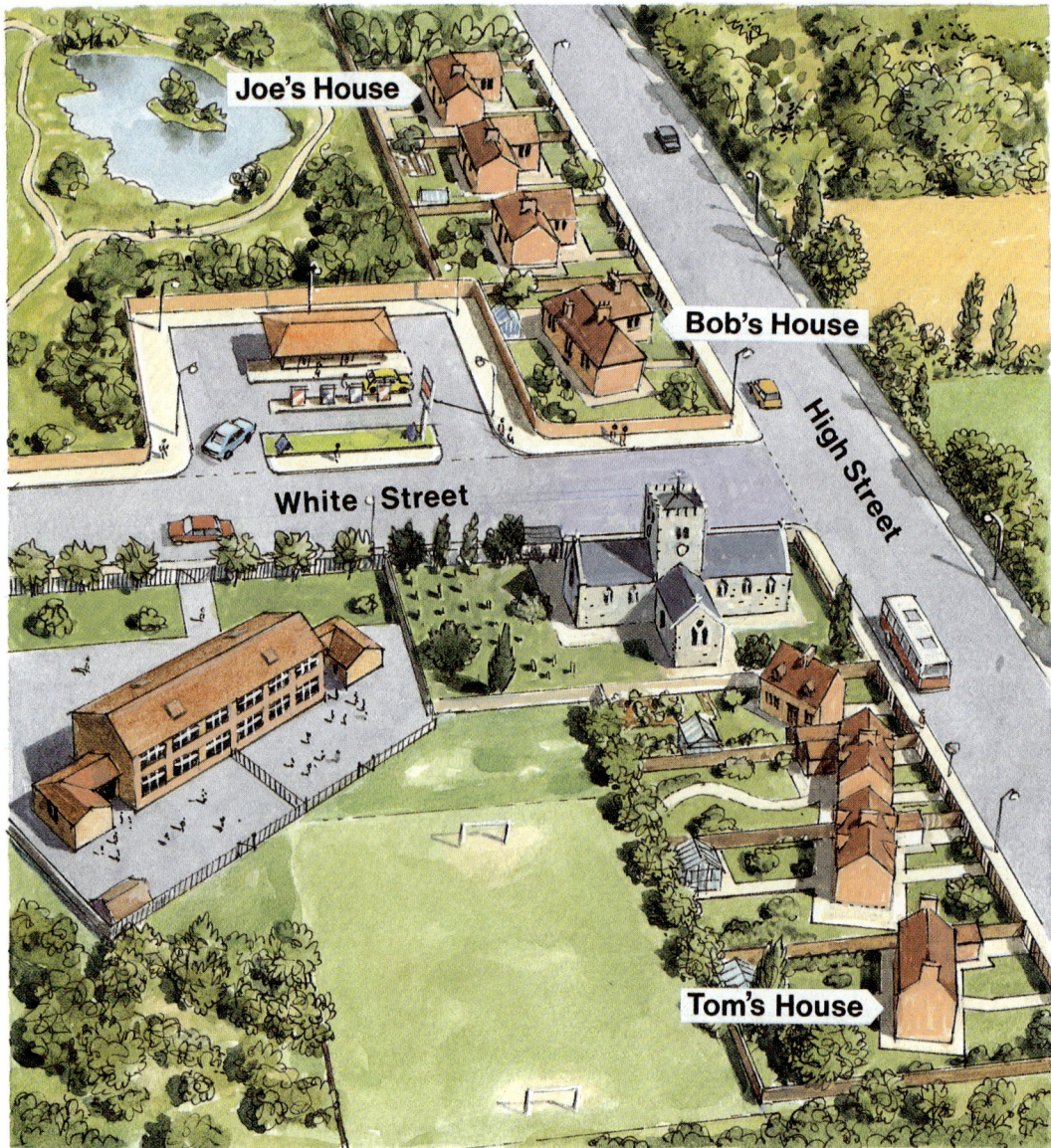

Joe's House

Bob's House

High Street

White Street

Tom's House

Tom, Bob and Joe all live in the High Street.

They go to the school in White Street.

Tom walks past 3 houses and a **church** and arrives at Bob's house.

Joe walks past 2 houses and arrives at Bob's house.

All three walk up White Street.

They pass the **petrol station** before they reach the **school**.

Look again at the picture and then at this map.

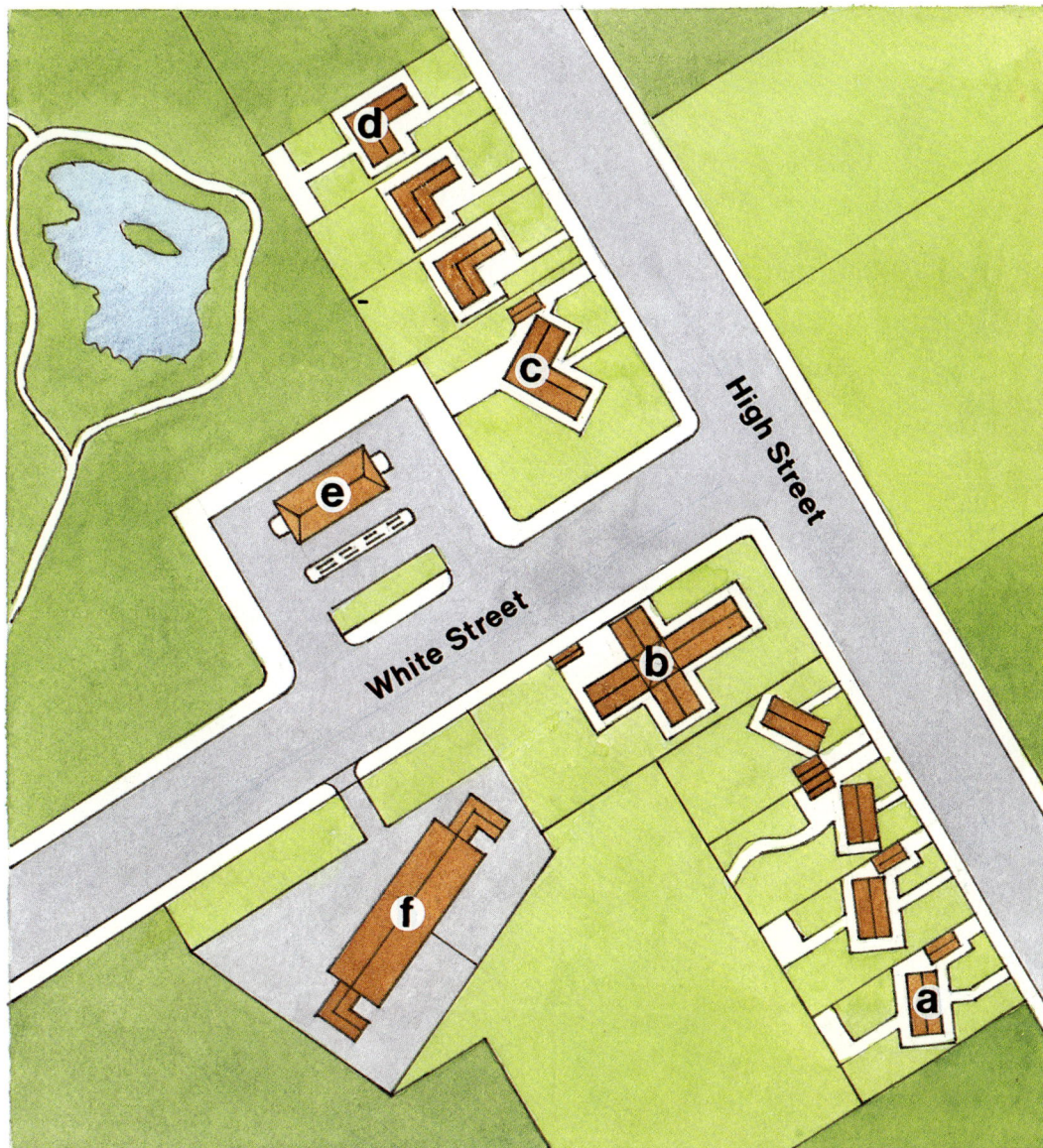

1. What is (a) on the map?
2. What is (b) on the map?
3. What is (c) on the map?

4. What is (d) on the map?
5. What is (e) on the map?
6. What is (f) on the map?

5. Step by Step

Sequences

Zena catches a cold

Below are two pictures. They are in the order (a), (b).

Which do you think is the correct order?

Is it   (a) (b)?

or   (b) (a)?

(a)   (b)

Jane takes the dog for a walk

What is the correct order of these three pictures?

(a)
Fido starts to
chase a cat.

(b)
The cat climbs
up a tree.

(c)
Jane sets off
with Fido.

1. What happened first? Was it (a), (b) or (c)?
2. What happened second? (a), (b) or (c)?
3. What happened third?   (a), (b) or (c)?

More pictures and sentences to put in order

She turns on the tap.

She washes her hands in soapy water.

Myra's hands are covered with paint.

Myra dries her clean hands.

Write the sentences in the correct order.

Instructions

How to make a puppet

The pictures show you how to make a puppet. They are in the right order.

The instructions also tell you how to make a puppet. They are **not** in the right order.
Match the instructions with the picture.

1. Which instruction matches picture 1? *Answer:* (b)
2. Which instruction matches picture 2?
3. Which instruction matches picture 3?

Pictures

1.

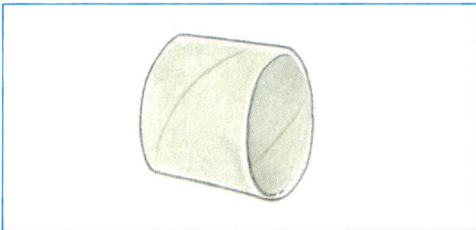

2.

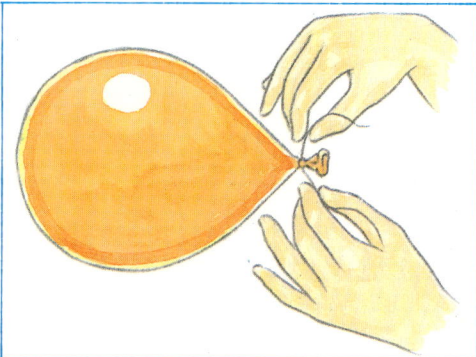

3.

Instructions

(a) Place the head on top of the neck.

(b) Get a piece of cardboard tube for a neck.

(c) Blow up a balloon for a head and tie the neck so that no air can get out.

4. Which instruction matches picture 4? *Answer:* (e)
5. Which instruction matches picture 5?
6. Which instruction matches picture 6?
7. Which instruction matches picture 7?

Pictures

Instructions

4.
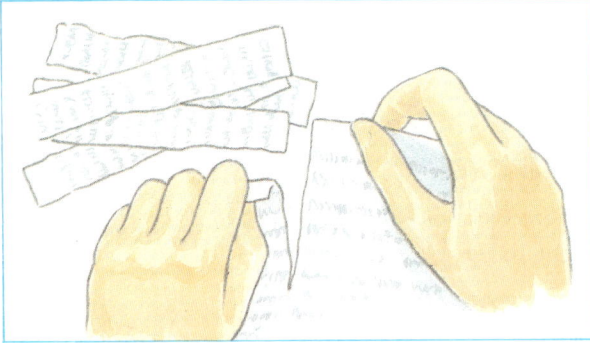

(d) Paint a face and hair on the puppet.

5.

(e) Cut up many strips of paper.

6.

(f) Get paste and a brush.

7.
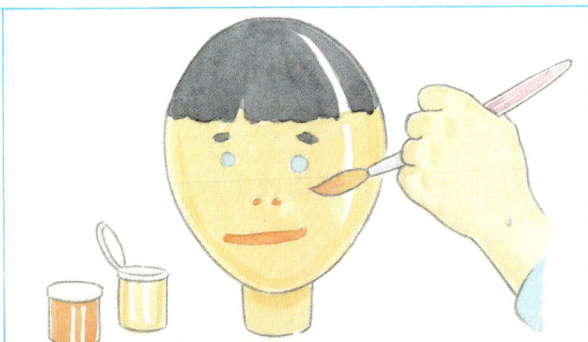

(g) Paste strips of paper. Stick them to the head and neck. Cover the head and neck 10 times with strips of pape

Secret Writing

Below are five sentences : (a), (b), (c), (d) and (e).
Read the sentences and then answer the questions below.

(a) You could write a secret message; one of the ways this can be done is to write, not with ink, but with lemon juice.

(b) You will need a pen with a nib, a sheet of paper and some lemon juice.

(c) Dip the pen nib in the lemon juice and write a message on the white paper.

(d) Allow it to dry and the message will disappear.

(e) To make it appear again, heat it near a light bulb.

Number 1 is done for you.

1. Which sentence tells you what to use instead of ink? *Answer:* (a)
2. Which sentence tells you what you need?
3. Which sentence tells you what happens when it is allowed to dry?
4. Which sentence tells you how to make the writing appear again?
5. Which sentence tells you how to write the message?

6. Clues

Picture clues

Look at pictures (a) and (b).
Look for clues to help you to work out the answers.

(a)   (b)

1. In picture (a) is Tom playing tennis or table tennis? Which clues made you choose your answer?
2. In picture (b) is Jean playing tennis or table tennis? Which clues made you choose your answer?

Look at the four pictures (a), (b), (c) and (d).

(a)

(b)

(c)

(d)

1. Which picture shows television filming?
   Is it (a), (b), (c) or (d)? Which clues did you see?
2. Which picture shows lessons outdoors? Which clues did you
   see?
3. Which pictures shows fishing? Which clues did you see?
4. Which picture shows canoeing? Which clues did you see?

Pictures and words

A picture can help to make a story more interesting and it can help to explain what we are reading.

Example: **The sheep shearing**

When Tom was in Australia he went to the sheep shearing. He saw the sheep being rounded up. Next the shearers set to work. The fleeces were stacked up in piles.

The picture helps us to guess what we will be reading about.

Write the answers in your own book.

Fill in the blanks.

Remember to look at the picture.

How we use water

1. We need water for _____.

2. We can travel by _____ wherever there is enough water.

3. We can put out ____ by using water.

4. To make plants grow in dry weather we must _____them.

5. We need water to wash.

Draw your own picture for 5.

Pictures can tell a story.

Pictures (a), (b) and (c) each tell us a story. Look at each picture. Write a story about it. Tell how it might end.

(a)

(b)

(c)